WEDDING MUSIC

I. ARIA

Viola
B-458

G. F. HANDEL

©Copyright 1990 by Southern Music Company, San Antonio, Texas 78292
International copyright secured. Printed in U.S.A. All rights reserved.

II. BRIDAL CHORUS

R. WAGNER

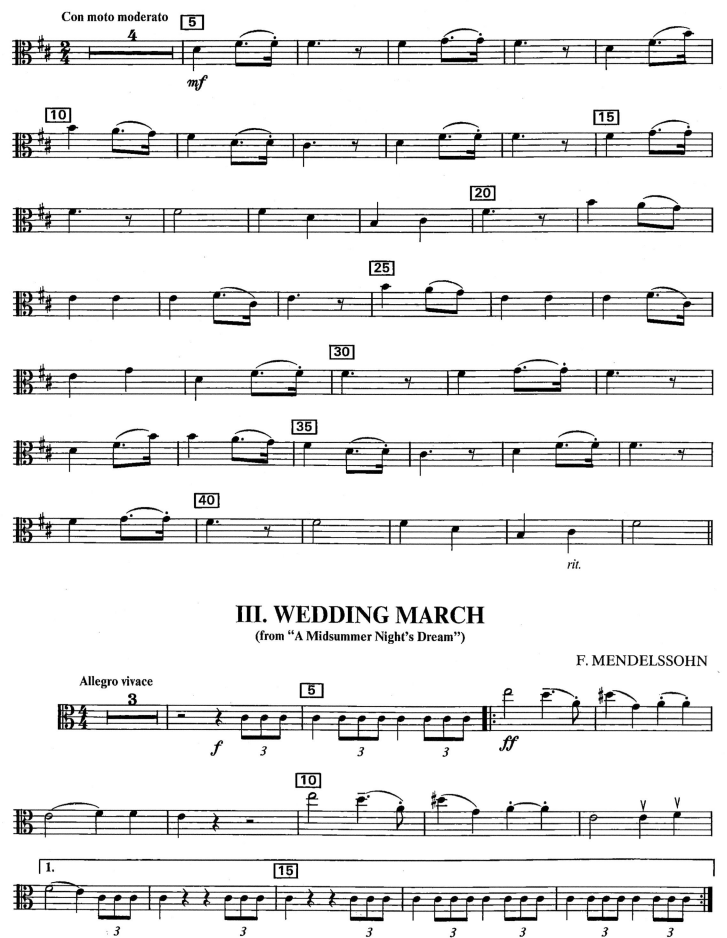

III. WEDDING MARCH
(from "A Midsummer Night's Dream")

F. MENDELSSOHN

IV. TRUMPET VOLUNTARY

J. CLARK

V. WINTER
(slow movement)

A. VIVALDI

VI. RIGAUDON

A. CAMPRA

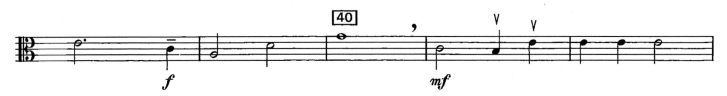

VII. THEME FROM 1ST SYMPHONY

J. BRAHMS

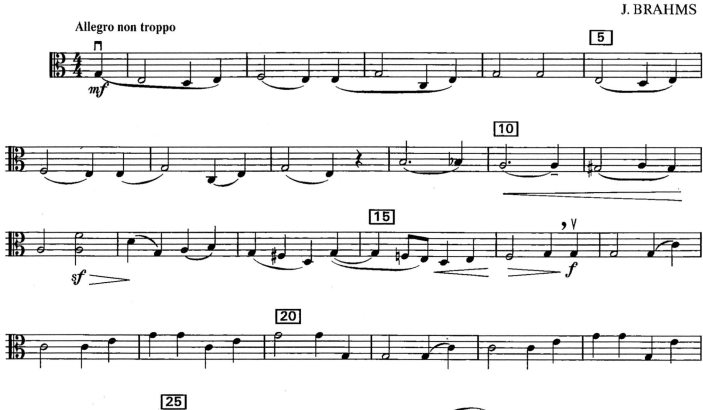

Viola

VIII. MARCH
(from "Marriage of Figaro")

W.A. MOZART

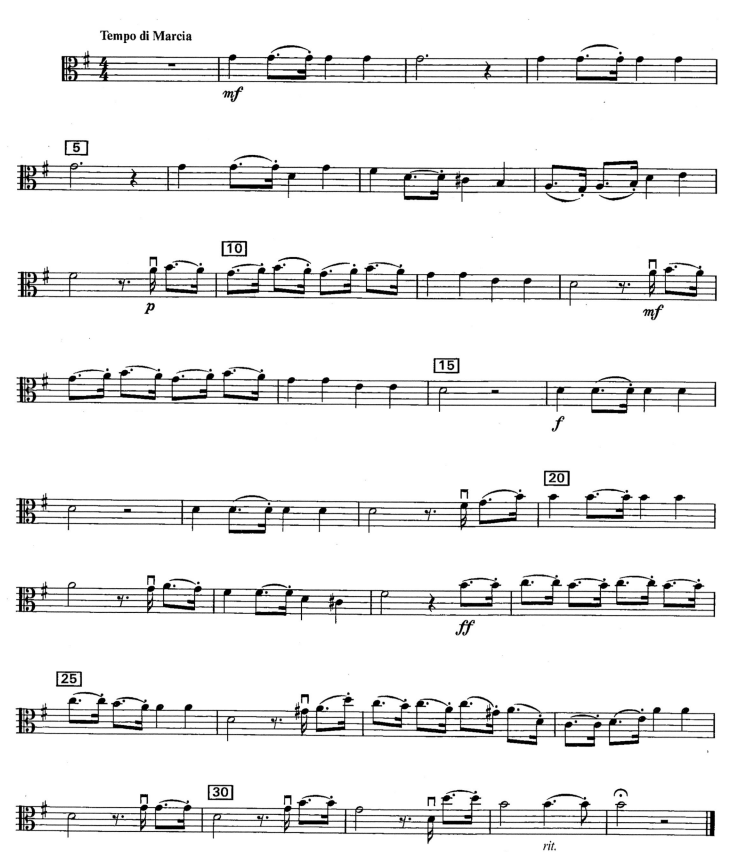

IX. TRUMPET TUNE

H. PURCELL

X. CANON

J. PACHELBEL

rit.

XI. JESU, JOY OF MAN'S DESIRING

J. S. BACH

poco rit.

B-458

XII. WINTER
(From 1st movement)

A. VIVALDI